CW00429001

To...........

From...................

Purple Ronnie's SECRET SANTA

First published 2010 by Boxtree
an imprint of Pan Macmillan, a division of Macmillan Publishers Limited
Pan Macmillan, 20 New Wharf Road, London N1 9RR
Basingstoke and Oxford
Associated companies throughout the world
www.panmacmillan.com

ISBN 978-0-7522-2722-1

Copyright © Purple Enterprises Ltd, a Coolabi company 2010

All rights reserved. No part of this publication may be
reproduced, stored in or introduced into a retrieval system, or
transmitted, in any form, or by any means (electronic, mechanical,
photocopying, recording or otherwise) without the prior written
permission of the publisher. Any person who does any unauthorized
act in relation to this publication may be liable to criminal
prosecution and civil claims for damages.

9 8 7 6 5 4 3 2 1

A CIP catalogue record for this book is
available from the British Library.

Printed and bound in Hong Kong

'Purple Ronnie' created by Giles Andreae. The right of Giles Andreae and Janet Cronin
to be identified respectively as the author and illustrator of this work has been asserted by them
in accordance with the Copyright, Designs and Patents Act 1988.

Visit www.panmacmillan.com to read more about all our books
and to buy them. You will also find features, author interviews and
news of any author events, and you can sign up for e-newsletters
so that you're always first to hear about our new releases.

a poem about

Secret Santa

A Secret Santa gift can
be

A tricky thing to choose:

Perfume, chocolate, music,
books –

Or if you're stuck, get
booze!

a poem about

Opening THAT Present

When you get it open
Don't roll your eyes and
sigh.
Say, "Thank you, Auntie,
very much.
What a lovely tie!"

a poem about

Christmas Baubles

My girlfriend sweetly asked
me

To decorate the tree

So I went and got my
baubles out

for all the world to see !

a poem about

Christmas Dinner

To get through Christmas Dinner

Here's the handiest of tips

Glug that bottle down your
throat

Don't mess about with sips

Daddy, Daddy! Uncle Peter and Auntie Mabel and Granny and Grandad and Fluffy and cousin Ethel are here!
!
tug

Why do they always
show The Great Escape
at Christmas?
Perhaps they're trying
to tell us something

a poem about the

Christmas Party

At the Christmas party
Be careful who you snog
Cos you might just pull
          a minger

While you're legless in the bog!

a poem to say

Merry Christmas

I hope that Santa brings you
Loads of smashing treats
and chocs
And not another sweater
Or a silly pair of socks!

a poem about

Christmas Pudding

You may think turkey, spuds
and sprouts
Are quite a heavy load
But leave some room for
pudding
Or your bottom might explode!

a poem about Christmas

Parties

At Christmas I like partying

And singing festive songs

Eating loads of splendid
nosh

And snogging all night long

<u>Top Tip</u>:

Give the booze a rest after Boxing Day. Prepare for New Year's Eve!

a poem about

Christmas Booze

Mix some wicked cocktails

Make them nice and strong

Then have a groovy

Christmas

And party all night long!

a poem about
Chrimbo Grub

Stuff your face with scrumptious grub

Cos Christmas time is here

And forget about the diet—

You can leave it till next year!

mega feast
yummy!
stuff
...mmm
bulge
triple choc fancies
nuts
sausage rolls
luxury trifle
crisps

a poem about

Party Time

Ho-Ho! It's Christmas Party
time
When most of us drink lots
And hope to snog those
workmates
Who've been giving us the hots!

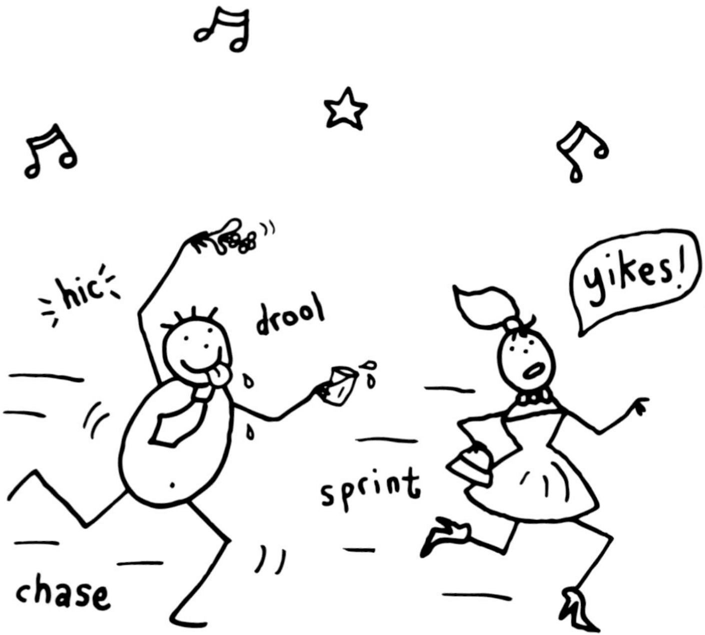

hic
drool
yikes!
sprint
chase

Christmas Dosh

The best thing there is
about Christmas
Except for good telly and
nosh
Is opening presents from family
and friends
That are stuffed full of packets
of dosh

a poem about
Christmas Cake

Years ago, when Gran was
                    young
She baked a cake and tinned
                        it
She's iced it up for Christmas
                      Day
Perhaps she should have
               binned it?

a poem about

Boxing Day

I sometimes wake on Boxing
Day

And feel I've fought a bout

With Whiskey, Gin and Vodka

And they've gone and knocked
me out!

a poem about a

Message to Santa

If you don't give me loads
of stuff
You know I'm not a joker
I'll chase you up the chimney
With a steaming red hot
poker!

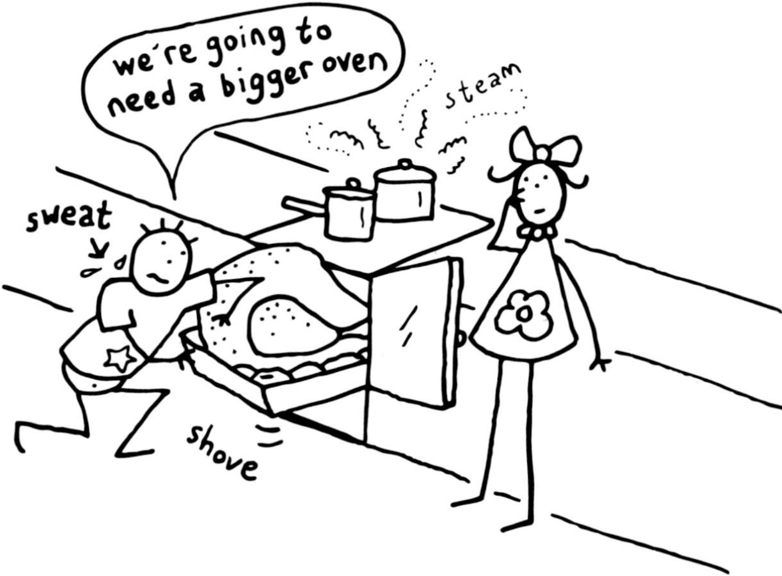
we're going to need a bigger oven
steam
sweat
shove

a poem about

Choosing The Turkey

Your Christmas Turkey should
be big
But make sure that you're
able
To fit it in the oven
Or get it on the table!

a poem about a

Great Present

At Christmas it's usually
hankies
Or a silly tasteless tie...
Well, blimey! It's posh
brandy!
I think I'm going to cry!

a poem about

Brussel Sprouts

Brussel sprouts are deadly

Cos you know that once you
start
There's just one thing they
lead to
A super-stinky fart!

Every Christmas brings more things for grandparents not to understand!

a poem about
Rubbish Presents

You hope to get an mp3

Or a snazzy mobile phone

But Christmas often brings
you gifts

That make you want to
groan!

a poem about

Mulberry Wine

I hope that you have a most
merry

And crazily wild Christmas
time
But don't let your face
Get lost without trace
In a vatful of mulberry
wine!

a poem about
Santa's Sherry

My mum puts out some sherry
For Santa and his elves
So I sneak down with
                    Neville
And we swig it all ourselves!

a poem about

Carol Singers

The carol singers offered me

Their box the other day

So I scooped out all the money

And I sent them on their way

a poem about
Christmas!

It isn't even light yet
You're bleary and you're
yawning
But the kids are bouncing
on your bed
"Yay! It's Christmas Morning!"

Santa's been!!
Get up!!
2 more minutes?!
it's Christmas DAY!
boing
boing
stamp
leap

a poem about

My Letter to Santa

I don't need ties or aftershave

So Santa, be a mate,
Bring me lots of lovely
beer
—if possible, a crate!

a poem about
Tinsel and Glitter

Nev put tinsel on his thing
To have a bit of fun
So I got purple glitter
And I stuck it on my bum!

We wish you a Merry Christmas
dazzle
twinkle
waggle
sparkle
ha ha!

a poem about the

Thank-you Grin

Practice in the mirror
On your instant thank-you
grin
Which hides the fact
you want to chuck
Some presents in the bin!

Purple Christmas

The man who said that Christmas
Should be white was off
                    his head
I'm going to have a rather
                    splendid

Purple one instead !

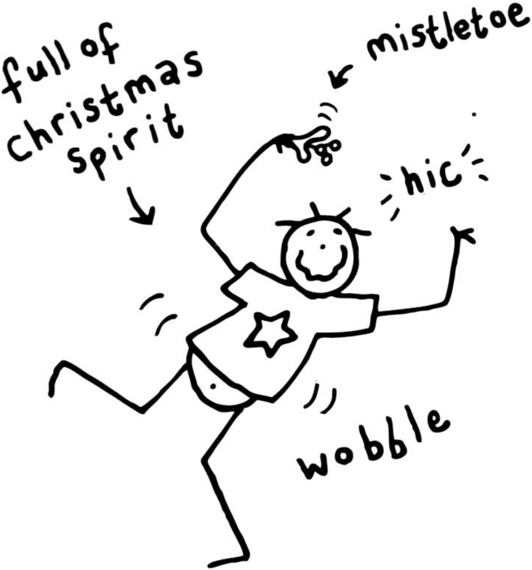
full of christmas spirit
mistletoe
hic
wobble